PHONICS BEGINNING CONSONANT BLENDS

READING BOOKS FOR 1ST GRADE

Children's Reading & Writing Books

This workbook will help you recognize words with consonant blends.

What What are Consonant Blends?

Consonant blends are groups of two or three consonants in a word that produce a consonant sound.

Let's get familiar with the consonants first with these "Words with Consonants" exercises.

Exercise no. 1

b as in bat

Write **b** if you hear the consonant sound /**b**/ as in **b**at.

1

bat   _ed   _at

2

_us   ha_   cra_

Name:_______________________

Exercise no. 2

c as in cat

Write **c** if you hear the consonant sound /**k**/ as in **cat**.

1   _cat   _ake   _un

2   _up   _en   _ap

Name:________________________

Exercise no. 3

d as in **d**og

Write **d** if you hear the consonant sound /**d**/ as in **d**og.

_dog   be__   __oor   **1**

ba__   __uck   sle__   **2**

Name: _______________________

Exercise no. 4

f as in fan

Write **f** if you hear the consonant sound /f/ as in **f**an.

1   f a n   _ i s h   e l _

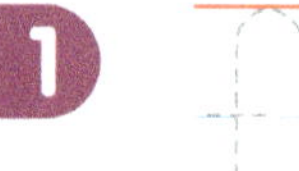

2   _ e a r   _ o o t   _ a s e

Name: _______________________________

Exercise no. 5

g as in goat

Write **g** if you hear the hard /**g**/ consonant sound as in **g**oat.

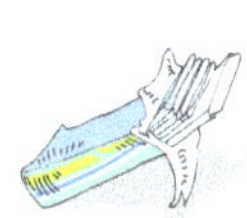

g̲um ̲oose bu̲ **1**

̲uitar pi̲ lio̲ **2**

Name:________________________________

Exercise no. 6

 **h as in hen**

Write **h** if you hear the consonant sound /**h**/ as in **h**en.

1 en __am __acht

2 __ouse __ouse __at

Name:_______________________________________

Exercise no. 7

 **j** as in **j**et

Write **j** if you hear the consonant sound /**j**/ as in **j**et.

▁jet ▁oat ▁am **1**

▁ump ▁ar ▁acket **2**

Name: _______________________________________

Exercise no. 8

k as in kite

Write **k** if you hear the consonant sound /**k**/ as in **k**ite.

1 
_k_ite boo__ __ump

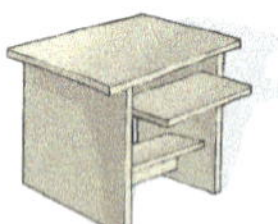  

2 des__ __ey __itten

Name:________________________________

Exercise no. 9

l as in lion

Write **l** if you hear the consonant sound /l/ as in lion.

1

lion   boa_   _eaf

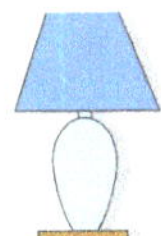  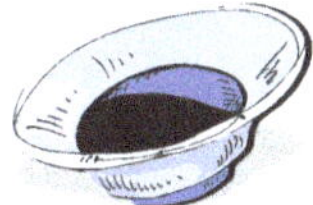

2

amp   boo   bow_

Name:________________________________

Exercise no. 10

 **m as in map**

Write **m** if you hear the consonant sound /**m**/ as in **m**ap.

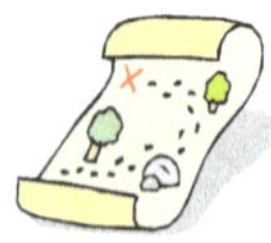  

1 __ap __oon __ut

2 __ose __ilk __ouse

Name:____

Exercise no. 11

n as in nut

Write n if you hear the consonant sound /n/ as in nut.

__ut   moo__   __est   **1**

__olf   lio__   __ouse   **2**

Name: _______________________________

Exercise no. 12

p as in pig

Write **p** if you hear the consonant sound /**p**/ as in **p**ig.

1  _pig   shee_   _ear

2 _oll   _each   _anda

Name:_______________________________________

Exercise no. 13

qu as in quilt

Write **qu** if you hear the sound /**kw**/ as in **qu**ilt.

1

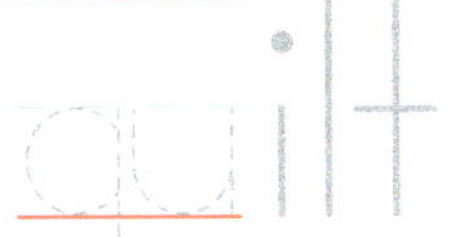quilt ___een ___ing

  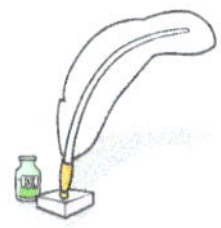

2

___ail ___ey ___ill

Name: _________________________________

Exercise no. 14

r as in rug

Write **r** if you hear the consonant sound /**r**/ as in **r**ug.

 **1** _rug   _an   _abbit

2 _un   _ose   _ose

Name:_______________________________________

Exercise no. 15

s as in sun

Write **s** if you hear the consonant sound /**s**/ as in **s**un.

_sun _ebra _anta **1**

eal bu _nake **2**

Name: _______________________

Exercise no. 16

t as in tub

Write **t** if you hear the consonant sound /**t**/ as in **t**ub.

 **1** tub   goa_   _urtle

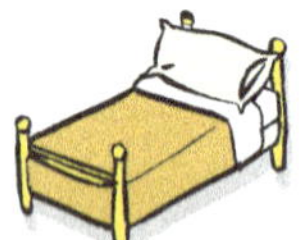  

2 be_   ba_   _able

Name: _______________________

Exercise no. 17

v as in vet

Write **v** if you hear the consonant sound /v/ as in **v**et.

   1

_v_et   _an   _an

    2

glo_e   el_   _iolin

Name:_______________________

Exercise no. 18

w as in web

Write **w** if you hear the consonant sound /**w**/ as in **w**eb.

1

 __web   __atch   __ig

2

__ater   __ __et   __ __et

Name: ____

x as in box

Write x if you hear the consonant sound /ks/ as in box.

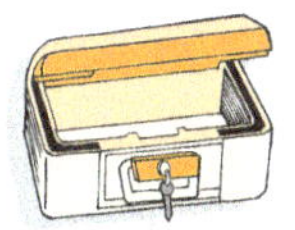

bo x

fo _

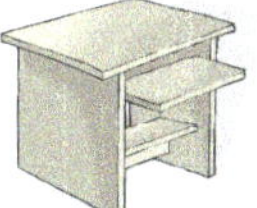

des _

1

6 ▶

si _

mi _

ca _

2

Name: _______________________

Exercise no. 20

y as in yak

Write y if you hear the consonant sound /y/ as in yak.

1  yak _o-yo _am

2 _awn _eal _ell

Name: _______________________

Exercise no. 21

z as in **z**oo

Write **z** if you hear the consonant sound /**z**/ as in **z**oo.

1

_zoo _ebra _ero

2

_eal bu__ _ipper

Name: _______________________________________

Consonant Blends
Reading and writing Exercises

Exercise no. 22

WRITE THE BEGINING CONSONANT BLENDS.

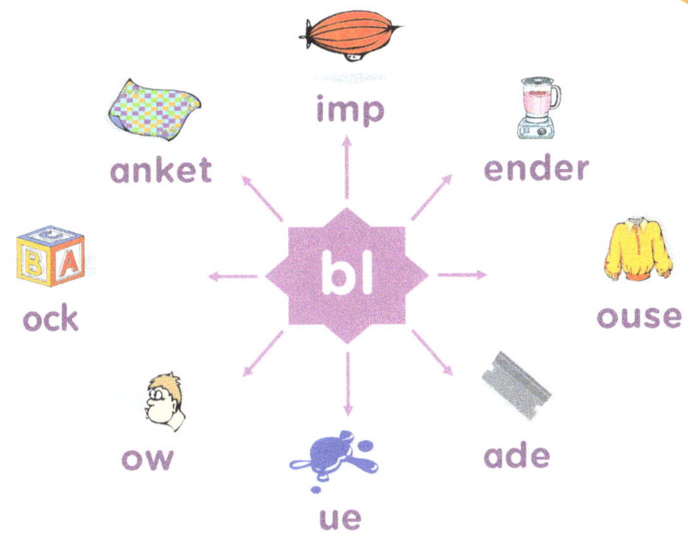

WRITE THE WORDS HERE:

Exercise no. 23

WRITE THE BEGINING CONSONANT BLENDS.

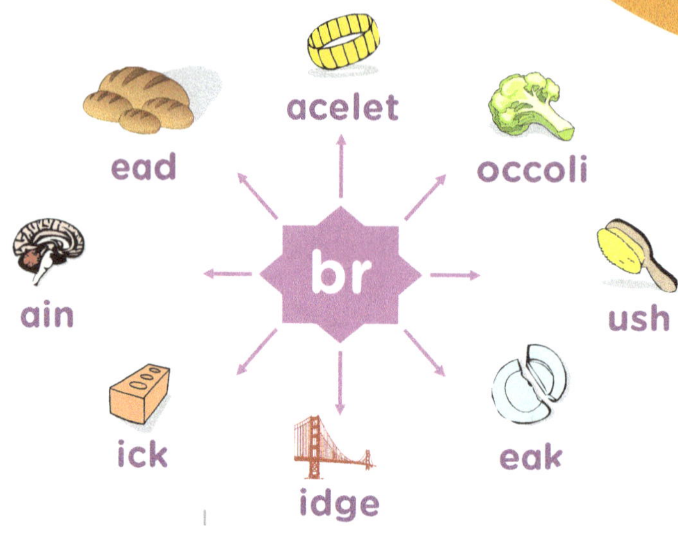

WRITE THE WORDS HERE:

Exercise no. 24

WRITE THE BEGINING CONSONANT BLENDS.

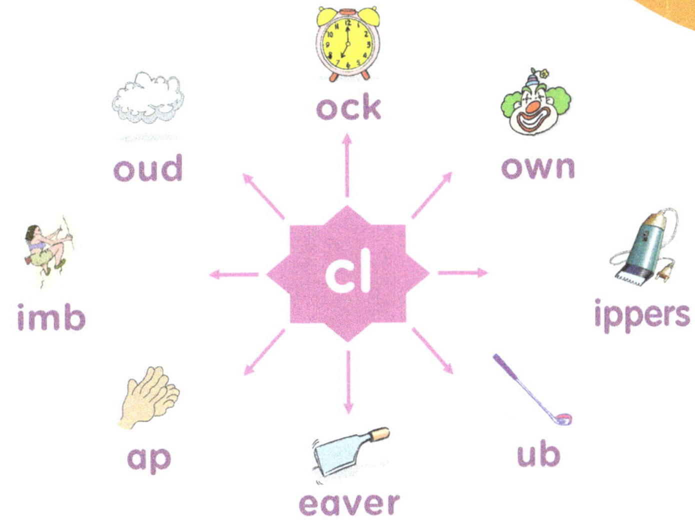

WRITE THE WORDS HERE:

Exercise no. 25

WRITE THE BEGINING CONSONANT BLENDS.

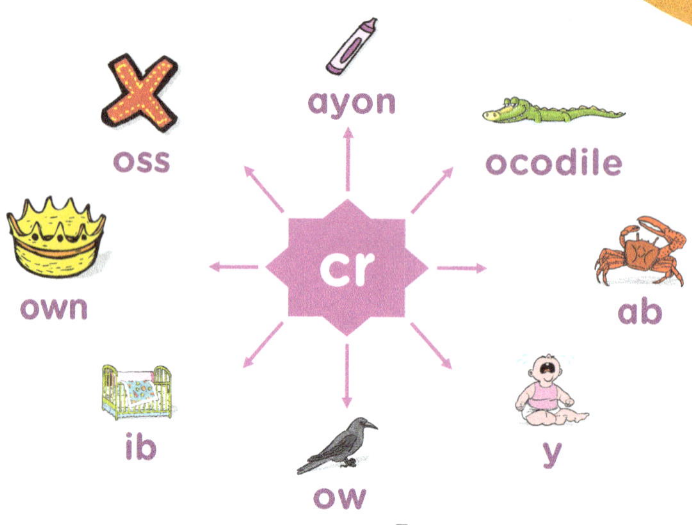

WRITE THE WORDS HERE:

WRITE THE BEGINING CONSONANT BLENDS.

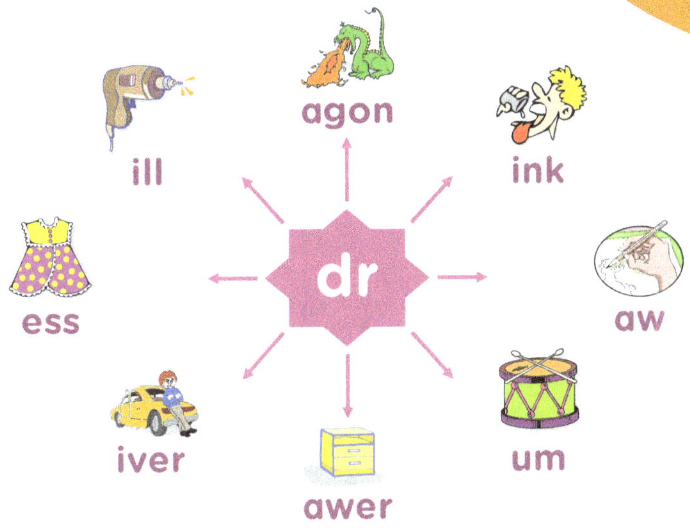

**WRITE THE WORDS HERE:

CIRCLE THE WORDS THAT CONTAIN THE CONSONANT BLEND BELOW:

br AND dr

WORDS YOU FOUND UNDER THE CORRECT CONSONANT BLEND COLUMN.

br-

brown
broun

dr-

drum
drəm

CIRCLE THE WORDS THAT CONTAIN THE CONSONANT BLEND BELOW:

bl AND tr

bl- block
bläk

tr- train
trān

CIRCLE THE WORDS THAT CONTAIN THE CONSONANT BLEND BELOW:

gr AND **sc**

W	F	G	I	M	S	B	P	M	K	F	P	Q	P	J
E	R	O	D	H	G	C	U	N	F	R	G	W	B	H
C	U	H	L	X	V	N	A	E	V	G	X	M	H	R
L	N	X	P	G	G	K	I	R	W	U	D	F	N	U
G	I	A	O	C	R	Q	Z	I	E	J	S	P	X	E
S	R	T	V	A	I	W	G	I	F	V	C	Y	C	B
R	U	O	Q	P	N	R	R	Z	G	Z	A	D	F	K
B	F	E	W	G	S	E	E	H	M	Z	R	H	W	P
T	W	N	O	I	C	A	E	M	Y	K	S	O	G	R
H	I	U	M	A	O	I	N	J	D	P	C	U	R	Y
I	R	Q	V	P	P	D	Y	I	Z	U	O	F	A	B
B	T	C	C	R	E	F	N	F	V	W	U	K	P	X
W	M	S	G	E	Q	E	G	V	V	O	T	V	E	Y
M	K	I	Z	B	O	W	B	G	T	S	Y	F	S	S
X	C	O	C	M	H	S	Z	D	L	S	D	J	Q	Z

gr- grass
gras

sc- scale
skāl

CIRCLE THE WORDS THAT CONTAIN THE CONSONANT BLEND BELOW:

gl AND **sk**

A	L	R	V	C	G	W	K	A	N	G	C	E	E	T
V	Q	M	P	T	N	A	D	W	S	L	E	L	P	N
G	E	W	M	K	L	U	I	S	K	A	P	U	W	F
D	E	S	K	I	L	L	Z	Q	Y	D	S	K	Z	Z
H	C	B	P	V	C	D	X	S	P	M	K	N	T	P
F	D	B	R	T	K	L	C	B	K	R	T	N	K	V
D	G	M	B	P	O	Y	C	V	X	E	P	I	Q	K
D	C	K	I	M	N	Z	V	O	A	Q	T	O	N	S
E	A	J	V	H	S	I	U	I	A	J	X	C	E	K
Q	C	H	E	C	L	T	B	Y	Z	G	G	K	H	U
B	W	G	L	E	A	M	V	H	R	M	L	K	B	L
A	T	C	L	M	B	I	Q	I	P	V	B	I	B	L
L	H	W	W	O	N	K	Y	E	V	M	F	A	D	D
L	F	V	M	M	W	R	O	Y	W	D	W	A	V	E
C	T	U	K	L	D	X	F	Z	T	Z	Y	U	G	N

WORDS YOU FOUND UNDER THE CORRECT CONSONANT BLEND COLUMN.

gl- glove
gləv

sk- skate
skāt

Exercise no. 31

CIRCLE THE WORDS THAT CONTAIN THE CONSONANT BLEND BELOW:

pr AND sl

WORDS YOU FOUND UNDER THE CORRECT CONSONANT BLEND COLUMN.

pr- pretzel
pretsəl

sl - slipper
ˈslipər

CIRCLE THE WORDS THAT CONTAIN THE CONSONANT BLEND BELOW:

pl AND sm

pl-   plug
       pləg

sm-   smock
       smäk

Exercise no. 33

pr or pl   sc or sk

 [ ] etzel    [ ] irt

 [ ] ug    [ ] ale

 [ ] ess    [ ] arf

 [ ] ane    [ ] hool

Name: _______________________

Exercise no. 34

br or bl   cr or cl

ock	ayon
ain	ock
own	oud
anket	ab

Name:_______________________

Exercise no. 35

fr or **fl**   **gr** or **gl**

[ ] ozen   [ ] obe

[ ] ag   [ ] ove

[ ] uit   [ ] ape

[ ] og   [ ] ocery

Name:_______________________

GOOD
JOB!

ANSWERS

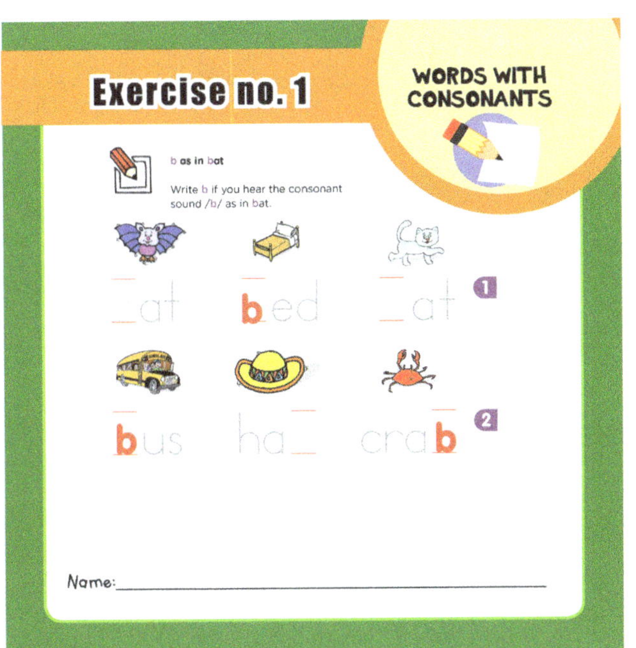

Exercise no. 1
WORDS WITH CONSONANTS
b as in bat
Write b if you hear the consonant sound /b/ as in bat.
_at   b ed   _at   1
bus   ha_   cra b   2
Name:_______________

Exercise no. 2
WORDS WITH CONSONANTS
c as in cat
Write c if you hear the consonant sound /k/ as in cat.
1   _at   c ake   _un
2   c up   _en   c ap
Name:_______________

Exercise no. 3
WORDS WITH CONSONANTS
d as in dog
Write d if you hear the consonant sound /d/ as in dog.
_og   be d   d oor   1
ba_   d uck   sle d   2
Name:_______________

Exercise no. 4
WORDS WITH CONSONANTS
f as in fan
Write f if you hear the consonant sound /f/ as in fan.
1   _an   f ish   el f
2   _ear   f oot   _ase
Name:_______________

Exercise no. 7
WORDS WITH CONSONANTS
j as in jet
Write j if you hear the consonant sound /j/ as in jet.
_et _oat jam 1
jump _ar jacket 2
Name:_______________

Exercise no. 6
WORDS WITH CONSONANTS
h as in hen
Write h if you hear the consonant sound /h/ as in hen.
1 _en ham _acht
2 house _ouse hat
Name:_______________

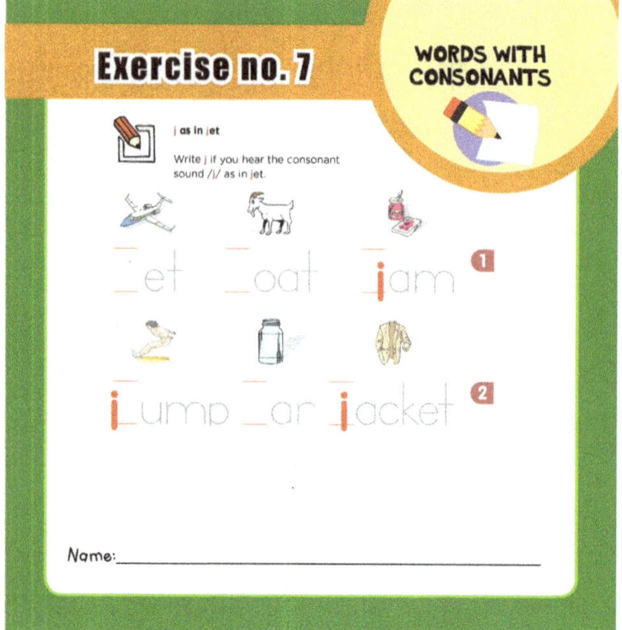
Exercise no. 7
WORDS WITH CONSONANTS
j as in jet
Write j if you hear the consonant sound /j/ as in jet.
_et _oat jam 1
jump _ar jacket 2
Name:_______________

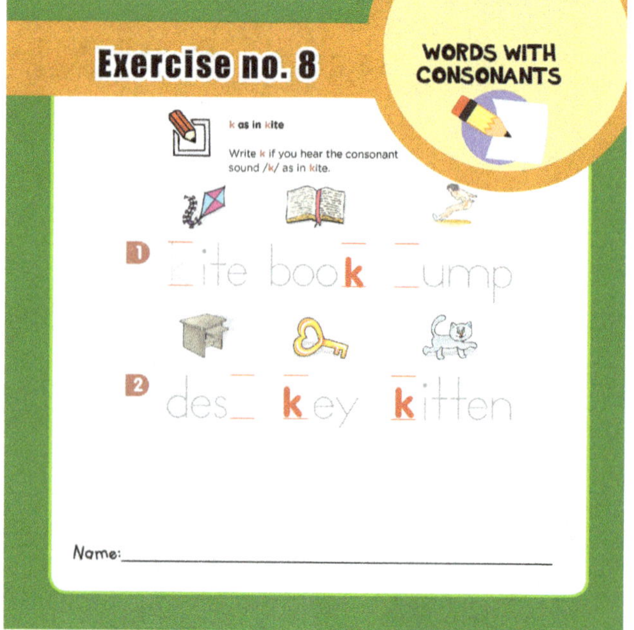
Exercise no. 8
WORDS WITH CONSONANTS
k as in kite
Write k if you hear the consonant sound /k/ as in kite.
1 _ite book _ump
2 des_ key kitten
Name:_______________

Exercise no. 9
WORDS WITH CONSONANTS
l as in lion
Write l if you hear the consonant sound /l/ as in lion.
1
ion boa _leaf
2
lamp boo bow_
Name:____________________

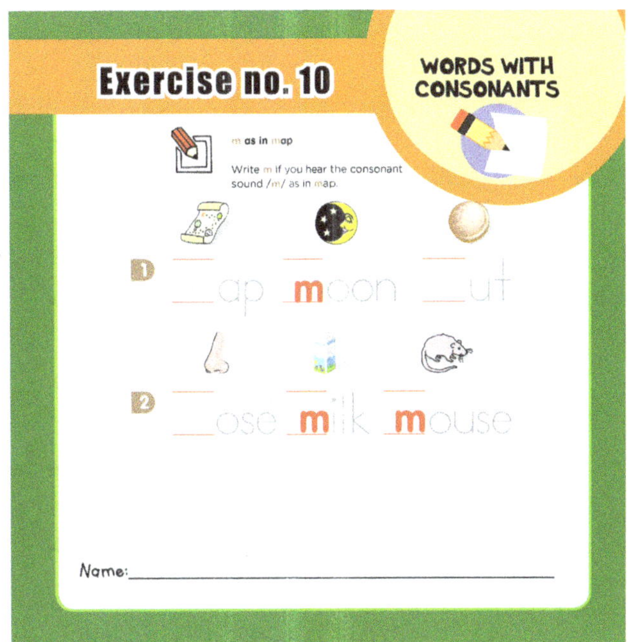

Exercise no. 10
WORDS WITH CONSONANTS
m as in map
Write m if you hear the consonant sound /m/ as in map.
1
_ap _moon _ut
2
_ose _milk _mouse
Name:____________________

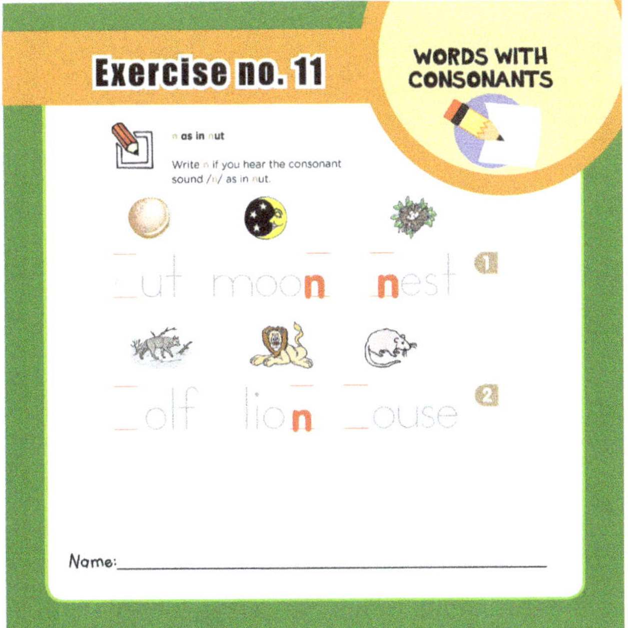

Exercise no. 11
WORDS WITH CONSONANTS
n as in nut
Write n if you hear the consonant sound /n/ as in nut.
1
ut moo _nest
2
olf lio _ouse
Name:____________________

Exercise no. 12
WORDS WITH CONSONANTS
p as in pig
Write p if you hear the consonant sound /p/ as in pig.
1
ig sheep _pear
2
_oll _peach _panda
Name:____________________

Exercise no. 13
WORDS WITH CONSONANTS
qu as in quilt
Write qu if you hear the sound /kw/ as in quilt.
_ilt   qu een   _ing   1
qu ail   _ey   qu ill   2
Name:______________________

Exercise no. 14
WORDS WITH CONSONANTS
r as in rug
Write r if you hear the consonant sound /r/ as in rug.
1   _ug   _an   r abbit
2   r un   r ose   _ose
Name:______________________

Exercise no. 15
WORDS WITH CONSONANTS
s as in sun
Write s if you hear the consonant sound /s/ as in sun.
_un   _ebra   s anta   1
s eal   bu s   s nake   2
Name:______________________

Exercise no. 16
WORDS WITH CONSONANTS
t as in tub
Write t if you hear the consonant sound /t/ as in tub.
1   _ub   goa_   t urtle
2   be_   ba t   t able
Name:______________________

Exercise no. 17
WORDS WITH CONSONANTS
v as in vet
Write v if you hear the consonant sound /v/ as in vet.
_et   van   _an   1
glove   el_   violin   2
Name:_______________

Exercise no. 18
WORDS WITH CONSONANTS
w as in web
Write w if you hear the consonant sound /w/ as in web.
1   _eb   watch   wig
2   water   wet   _et
Name:_______________

Exercise no. 19
WORDS WITH CONSONANTS
x as in box
Write x if you hear the consonant sound /ks/ as in box.
bo_   fox   des_   1
six   mix   ca_   2
Name:_______________

Exercise no. 20
WORDS WITH CONSONANTS
y as in yak
Write y if you hear the consonant sound /y/ as in yak.
1   _ak   yo-yo   _am
2   yawn   _eal   yell
Name:_______________

Exercise no. 21

Name:_______________________

Exercise no. 22

Write the begining consonant blends.

Write the words here:

blanket	blade
block	blouse
blow	blender
blue	blimp

Exercise no. 23

Write the begining consonant blends.

Write the words here:

bread	bridge
brain	break
brick	brush
bracelet	broccoli

Exercise no. 24

Write the begining consonant blends.

Write the words here:

climb	clippers
clap	clown
cleaver	clock
club	cloud

Exercise no. 25

Write the begining consonant blends.

Write the words here:

crib   crocodile

crow   crayon

cry   cross

crab   crown

Exercise no. 26

Write the begining consonant blends.

Write the words here:

drill   drum

dress   draw

driver   dragon

drawer   drink

Exercise no. 27

Circle the words that contains the consonant blend below:

br and **dr**

R	U	Q	X	O	V	R	Z	S	R	M	Y	R	U	T
M	Y	Q	B	F	R	D	T	O	M	U	K	O	C	W
G	V	O	G	U	F	E	P	O	R	Y	I	H	X	U
H	C	R	G	R	B	R	V	Z	B	B	R	I	N	G
B	D	H	N	G	E	Q	B	F	K	K	D	H	W	N
H	P	C	M	W	Y	A	D	M	E	B	K	E	A	V
T	D	M	M	V	U	D	I	M	R	Y	O	S	O	F
A	T	U	F	F	Z	B	H	Z	M	A	O	U	F	T
W	O	W	T	C	N	K	U	X	Y	I	X	Q	M	B
E	V	R	O	T	O	Y	K	S	N	Z	E	E	F	F
Z	O	T	Q	X	S	R	H	B	Y	T	P	D	R	F
M	F	D	F	V	W	H	O	O	N	Z	C	R	O	E
V	Z	A	W	V	L	W	X	O	X	O	I	K	W	W
B	G	A	F	J	L	C	L	F	L	C	O	L	E	E
S	O	V	S	P	S	Z	M	O	V	Y	R	L	K	F

Write the searched words under the same consonant blend column.

br- brown	dr- drum
bread	dry
bring	drive
brain	drill
broke	drop

Circle the words that contains the consonant blend below:

bl and **tr**

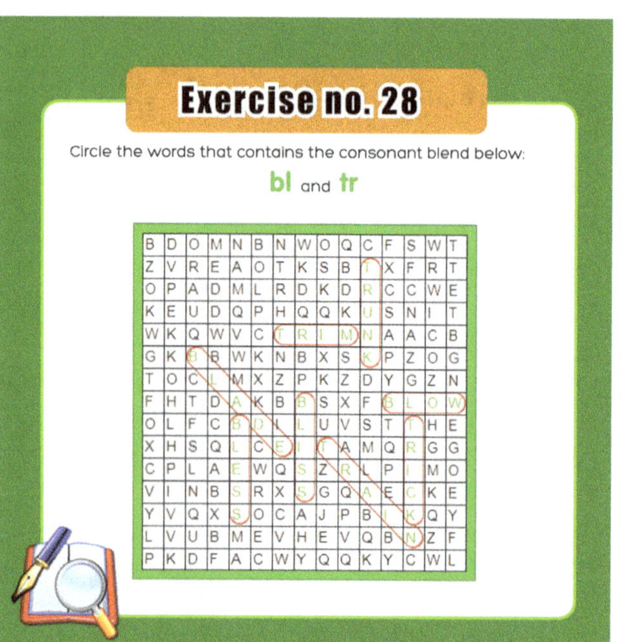

Write the searched words under the same consonant blend column.

bl- block bläk	tr- train trän
blow	trick
bless	train
bliss	trunk
blade	trim

Circle the words that contains the consonant blend below:

gr and **sc**

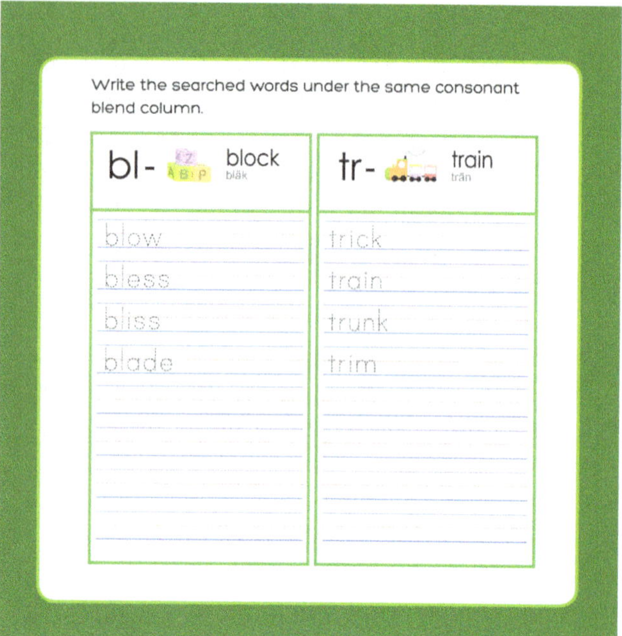

Write the searched words under the same consonant blend column.

gr- grass gras	sc- scale skäl
green	scare
grapes	scout
grin	scope
grow	scar

Exercise no. 30

Circle the words that contains the consonant blend below:

gl and sk

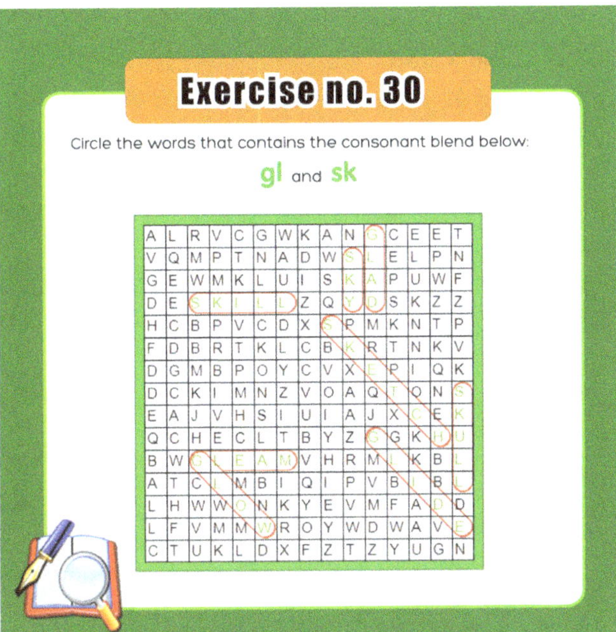

Write the searched words under the same consonant blend column.

gl- glove	sk- skate
glow	skill
glad	skull
glide	sky
gleam	sketch

Exercise no. 31

Circle the words that contains the consonant blend below:

pr and sl

Write the searched words under the same consonant blend column.

pr- pretzel	sl- slipper
prawn	slide
prunes	slow
prone	sled
prick	slam

Exercise no. 32

Circle the words that contains the consonant blend below:

pl and sm

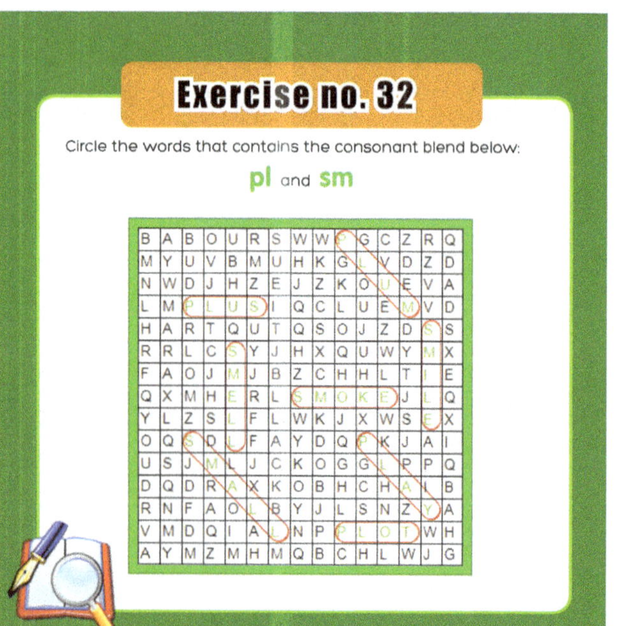

Write the searched words under the same consonant blend column.

pl- plug	sm- smock
plot	small
plus	smell
play	smoke
plum	smile

Exercise no. 33

pr or **pl**   **sc** or **sk**

- **pr** etzel
- **pl** ug
- **pr** ess
- **pl** ane

- **sk** irt
- **sc** ale
- **sc** arf
- **sc** hool

Name:_______________________

Exercise no. 34

br or **bl**   **cr** or **cl**

- **bl** ock
- **br** ain
- **br** own
- **bl** anket

- **cr** ayon
- **cl** ock
- **cl** oud
- **cr** ab

Name:_______________________

Exercise no. 35

fr or **fl**   **gr** or **gl**

- **fr** ozen
- **fl** ag
- **fr** uit
- **fr** og

- **gl** obe
- **gl** ove
- **gr** ape
- **gr** ocery

Name:_______________________

Visit

BABY PROFESSOR
EDUCATION KIDS

www.BabyProfessorBooks.com

to download Free Baby Professor eBooks
and view our catalog of new and exciting
Children's Books

www.ingramcontent.com/pod-product-compliance
Lightning Source LLC
Chambersburg PA
CBHW081713160726
47997CB00024B/2862